First published 1983 by Editions Gallimard
First published 1984 in Great Britain by
Moonlight Publishing Ltd,
131 Kensington Church Street, London W8
Illustrations © 1983 by Editions Gallimard
English text and selection of poems © 1984 by
Moonlight Publishing Ltd

Printed in Italy by La Editoriale Libraria

ISBN 0 907144 59 4

AUTUMN

DISCOVERERS

by Laurence Ottenheimer
adapted and edited by Alex Campbell
illustrations by Henri Galeron

MOONLIGHT PUBLISHING

But I thought not once of winter
Or summer that was past
Till I saw that slant-legged robin
With autumn on his chest.

Andrew Young

This book
belongs to

....

....

There are twelve months throughout
the year,
From January to December –
And the primest month of all the twelve
Is the merry month of September!
Then apples so red
Hang overhead,
And nuts ripe-brown
Come showering down
In the bountiful days of September!

There are flowers enough in the
summer-time,
More flowers than I can remember –
But none with the purple, gold, and red
That dye the flowers of September!
The gorgeous flowers of September!
And the sun looks through
A clearer blue,
And the moon at night
Sheds a clearer light
On the beautiful flowers of September!

Mary Howitt

September

Autumn begins at the autumn equinox. This is one of the two occasions in the year when day and night are of equal length. It occurs on 22 or 23 September. During autumn the days grow gradually shorter, until the end of the season on the shortest day of the year: the winter solstice, which occurs on 21 or 22 December.

22	Thirty days has September, April, June and November.
23	
24 **25**	September was called 'Harvest Month' by the Saxons.
26 **27** **28**	*A nip in the air today, and autumn Playing hide and seek with summer.* Leonard Clark
29	Michaelmas, the festival of St Michael and All Angels.
30	Michaelmas daisies are in bloom.

*Day by day
The sun's broad
   beam
Fades away
By a golden gleam;
– Hark on the cliff
How the sea-gulls
   scream!*
James Stephens

October

In early October the sun rises at about 6 o'clock and sets at about 17.40. Each day sunrise is a little under 2 minutes later and sunset 2 minutes earlier.

1
Hail, old October,
*   bright and chill*
> Thomas Constable

2

3
Evening red and morning grey,
Two sure signs of one fine day.

4

5
A good October and a good blast
To blow the hog acorn and mast.

6

7
8
9
The warm sun is failing,
The bleak wind is wailing,
The bare boughs are sighing,
The pale flowers are dying.
> P. B. Shelley

10
11
The Americans call Autumn
'the Fall', because it is the
season when leaves fall.

Fall, leaves, fall; die, flowers, away;
*   Lengthen night and shorten day;*
Every leaf speaks bliss to me
Fluttering from the autumn tree.   Emily Brontë

12

13 Thunder in October brings
good vintages.

14

15 *Now it is autumn and the falling*
fruit . . .
          D.H. Lawrence

16

17

18 Good weather around the 18th
is known as St Luke's little
19 summer.

20 In October dung your field
And your land its wealth shall
21 yield.

Intery, mintery,
*   cutery corn,*
Apple seed and
*   apple thorn;*
Wine, brier,
*   limber lock,*
Three geese in a
*   flock,*
One flew east, one
*   flew west,*
And one flew over
*   the cuckoo's*
*   nest.*
          Mother Goose
          counting rhyme

Shine on the kangaroo, thou sun!
Make far New Zealand faint with fear!
Don't hurry back to spoil our fun,
Thank goodness, old October's here! Thomas Constable

22
23
Fresh October brings the pheasant;
Then to gather nuts is pleasant
Sara Coleridge

24

25
26
Warm October, cold February. When birds and badgers are fat in October, expect a cold winter.

27

28
29
30
31
Hallowe'en is the eve of All Hallows' or All Saints' Day (1 November). Hallowe'en was thought to be the night when witches and spirits were on the loose. Placed in a window, hollowed out pumpkins lit up by a candle grin at the spooks outside.

They chose me from
my brother:
That's the Nicest
one, they said,
And they carved me
out a face and
put a
Candle in my head;

And they set me on
the doorstep.
Oh, the Night was
dark and wild,
But when they lit the
candle,
Then I smiled!

Dorothy Aldis

12

November

In early November the sun rises at about 6.50 and sets at about 16.35. Each day sunrise is a little under 2 minutes later and sunset a little over 1 minute earlier.

1 All Saints' Day

Since the seventh century 1 November has been set aside by the Christian Church to commemorate the saints.

2 All Souls' Day,
a day to remember the dead.

3
4
*The geese flying south
In a long row and v-shaped
Pulling in winter.*

Sally Andresen

5 Guy Fawkes Night

*Please to
    remember
The Fifth of
    November,
Gunpowder
    treason and
    plot;
I know no reason
Why gunpowder
    treason
Should ever be
    forgot.*

Anon.

Autumn wind rises; white clouds fly.
Grass and trees wither, geese go south.
Wu-Ti, Chinese Emperor

6

7 Ice in November
Brings mud in December.

8

9

10

11 Armistice Day.
The First World War ended
on 11 November 1918.

12

13 Clear autumn, windy winter;
Warm autumn, long winter.

14

15
16 'Tween Martinmas and Yule
Water's wine in every pool.
Scottish proverb

17

18 Thunder in November, a
fertile year to come.

*In autumn when
the woods are
red
And skies are grey
and clear,
The sportsmen
seek the wild
fowl's bed
Or follow down
the deer.*
R.L. Stevenson

No shade, no shine, no butterflies, no bees,
No fruits, no flowers, no leaves, no birds.
No-vember! Thomas Hood

19

20
Dull November brings the blast;
21
Then the leaves are whirling fast.
Sara Coleridge

22
St Cecilia, patron saint of musicians.

23

24
Like birds unfledged and young,
25
The old bare branches cry;
Branches that shake and bend
To feel the winds go by.
W.H. Davies

26

27
The fourth Thursday in November is Thanksgiving Day in the USA.

28

29
Much fog in autumn, much snow in winter.

30
St Andrew, patron saint of Scotland.

I like the gray November day, And bare dead boughs That coldly sway Against my pane. I like the rain.
Dixie Wilson

15

December

In early December the sun rises at about 7.40 and sets at about 15.55. Each day sunrise is about 1 minute later, sunset 1 minute earlier, until the winter solstice.

1
2
October, November, December,
Glow, like an ember,
Roast, warm as toast,
Heat your feets, under the sheets.
Geoffrey Summerfield

3

4 December cold with snow, good for rye.

5

6 St Nicholas's Day

St Nicholas, or Santa Claus, is the Father Christmas of many northern countries. He used to leave presents in children's shoes, but naughty children might have found themselves threatened with a beating instead.

7 On St Ambrose's Day cold weather comes for eight days.

8

Chill December brings the sleet,
Blazing fire and Christmas treat.
Sara Coleridge

9

10 *It's autumn, autumn, autumn late,*
'Twill soon be winter snow.
William Allingham

11

12

13 St Lucy's Day

14

15

16

17 *This is the week when Christmas comes,*
Let every pudding burst with plums.
Eleanor Farjeon

18

19

20 St Thomas grey, St Thomas grey,
Longest night and shortest day.

21

In Sweden girls wear crowns of candles on St Lucy's Day, Sankt Lucia in Swedish, the festival of light. The name Lucy comes from the Latin word *lux*, meaning 'light'.

17

Days and seasons

Summer's sun is warm and bright,
Winter's snow is cold and white,
Autumn brings the sheaves of grain,
Spring will scatter flowers again;
Pleasant changes
God arranges
All throughout the year!

First there's darkness then there's light,
First we've day and then we've night,
First we're hot and then we're cold,
First we're young and then we're old;
Are we knowing
Where we're going,
What we're doing here?

Jane Euphemia Browne

The autumn equinox

We have day and night because, as well as orbiting around the sun, the Earth is constantly spinning on its axis, an imaginary line from the North Pole to the South Pole. It takes the Earth 24 hours to spin round once on its axis. During that time it is day in the part of the Earth nearest the sun, and receiving its light, and night on the other side of the Earth, which is in shadow. The Earth is slightly tilted on this imaginary line, which means that day and night are usually of different lengths. But twice a year, in autumn and in spring, day and night last the same length of time: 12 hours each. And these two periods are called the equinoxes. The autumn equinox marks the beginning of autumn when the days begin to grow shorter.

Every hour the Earth travels about 107,220 kilometres (66,620 miles), and it takes the Earth a year to complete its orbit around the sun. We have seasons because different parts of the Earth are nearer the sun during this orbit.

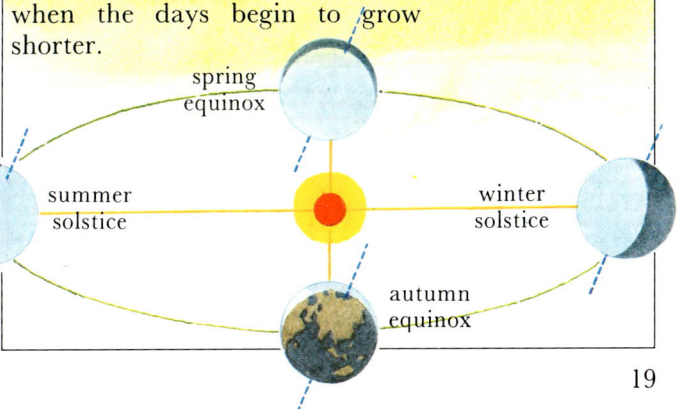

spring
equinox

summer
solstice

winter
solstice

autumn
equinox

Stars in the autumn sky

1 Hercules
2 The Wagoner
3 The Great Bear
4 The Charioteer
5 Perseus
6 Cassiopeia
7 Cepheus
8 The Little Bear
9 Draco – the
  Dragon

Groups of stars are called constellations and, viewed from Earth, many of these constellations seem to form patterns and pictures. For this reason, in ancient times, each known constellation was named after mythical people or creatures.

The constellations we can see change from season to season, because the Earth revolves around the sun. Here are two views of the night sky that can be seen from Europe in early autumn.

**Looking
north**

20

*I never see the stars at night
  waltzing round the moon
without wondering why they dance when
  no one plays a tune.*

George Barker

The Ancient Greeks had legends for most constellations they could see.

Perseus, the son of Zeus, is a Greek hero who flew on winged sandals. He saved the princess Andromeda from a sea-monster. And she and her parents queen Cassiopeia and king Cepheus are not far from Perseus in the sky.

1 The Fishes
2 The Whale
3 The Water-Bearer
4 The Goat
5 The Archer
7 The Eagle
8 The Dolphin
9 The Winged Horse

Looking south

Dew and mist

After a warm autumn day followed by a cold night we often wake to find the grass scattered with little drops of water, although it has not rained. They are dew drops.

The air is partly composed of water vapour. Warm air can hold more vapour than cold; so, when air is cooled at night, the excess vapour condenses into drops and falls to the ground as dew.

Mist is a low cloud that forms when the air close to the ground contains a lot of water vapour and is suddenly cooled. The vapour then condenses into tiny drops of water that are too light to fall.

Because river-fog
Hiding the mountain base
Has risen,
The autumn mountain looks as
though it hung in the sky.

Fukayaba Kiyowara

White frost, black ice

Black ice is one of the most dangerous road conditions of all because, despite its name, it is almost invisible.

As autumn advances, it brings frost and ice.

A white frost occurs when dew drops freeze to form ice crystals on plants, grasses, dead leaves, twigs . . .

Black ice forms on the road when its surface is cold enough to freeze water vapour in any damp winds blowing over it. The vapour turns into a hard sheet of ice on the road's surface.

Fog and rime

Fog is a thick mist. It forms most often over open country where there are lakes or rivers from which the air draws water vapour.

When fog freezes, it covers grass, trees and anything else it touches in a fine coat of ice crystals. This is rime.

A hill full, a hole full,
Yet you cannot catch a bowl full.

Answer:
Mist

I saw the fog grow thick,
Which soon made blind my ken;
It made tall men of boys,
And giants of tall men . . .

The street lamps, and the lights
Upon the halted cars,
Could either be on earth
Or be the heavenly stars.

W.H. Davies

Trees in autumn

As autumn days grow colder and night falls earlier, trees prepare for their winter rest.

Deep under the ground the tree's roots are protected from frost and ice; but during cold weather they draw less water from the earth. Soon sap, which is water mixed with food, ceases to rise from the roots and circulate through the trunk and branches. The sap will rise again in the spring.

Meanwhile leaves of deciduous trees are losing their green. While days are long, leaves make plenty of green chlorophyll, which works with the light of the sun to make food for the tree out of water and carbon dioxide in the air. But without enough sun the chlorophyll starts to break down. Leaves turn red, yellow, brown or orange according to their kind.

> *Down, down!*
> *Yellow and brown*
> *The leaves are falling over the town.*
>
> Eleanor Farjeon

At the base of the stalk that holds each leaf to its branch, grows a cork-like layer, cutting the leaf off from the rest of the tree. The leaf no longer receives sap, and so it withers, dies and is blown off by the wind or falls under its own weight.

A few well-anchored leaves manage to hang on to the tree throughout the winter, until new leaves push them off in the spring.

Leaves fall,
Brown leaves,
Yellow leaves streaked with
brown.
They fall,
Flutter,
Fall again.
The brown leaves
And the streaked yellow leaves
Loosen on their branches
And drift slowly downward.

Amy Lowell

Autumn leaves

Leaves left on the ground will eventually rot to become humus, which makes the soil around the tree richer and helps it and other nearby plants to grow. Before this happens, try to collect different leaves and identify them, noticing which colours the leaves from different types of tree turn.

Ash

Aspen

Beech

Maple

Wild cherry

Willow

Chestnut

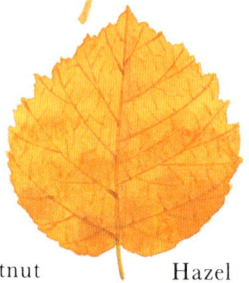

Hazel

*I know the beech has got its
    red,
I know the lime has got its
    gold,
And bracken is a tawny bed,
And dawn is white with mist,
    and cold.*

Eleanor Farjeon

Rowan tree

Horse chestnut

Poplar

Birch

Oak

Lime

Hornbeam

The age of a tree

Each year a tree grows a layer of new wood just beneath its bark. It stops growing as soon as sap ceases to flow in the autumn.

You can tell a tree's age when it has been felled by counting the annual layers, which appear as a series of rings across its trunk.

A wide ring of pale spring wood that carried a heavy flow of sap is always followed by a narrow dark ring of summer wood formed at the end of the growing season.

A ring of spring wood and a ring of summer wood together represent one year's growth. The rings that grew in a wet year will both be wider than those from a dry year.

Listen . . .
With faint dry sound,
Like steps of passing ghosts,
The leaves, frost-crisped,
Break from the trees
And fall.

Adelaide Crapsey

Inside the tree-trunk

Over the years, the wood at the centre of a tree-trunk hardens and dies. This is known as the tree's *heartwood* and it gives the tree its strength. The heartwood is darker in colour and rots easily if exposed to the air; when this happens, the tree becomes hollow.

The living wood surrounding the heartwood is known as the *sapwood* because the sap flows up through it to carry nourishment to the tree's branches and leaves. The sap completes its circulation through the tree by flowing back down through the *phloem*, or inner bark, now carrying food made by the leaves to the rest of the tree. This food enables new wood to grow. New wood and new phloem are made by the *cambium*, a very fine layer of soft wood lying between the sapwood and phloem.

1 Heartwood
2 Sapwood
3 Phloem
4 Bark

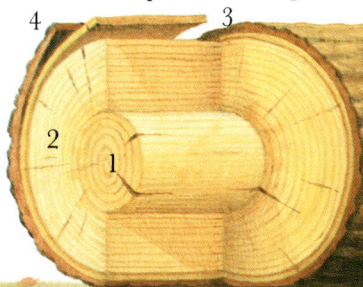

Trees and their bark

Bark shields a tree from attack by insects, fungi and the weather. It stops the sap from drying up in summer and from freezing in winter. Bark itself is dead wood.

When young, trees have thin, smooth bark. As a tree grows the bark splits and new bark forms underneath. Over the years the bark of a tree develops a pattern by which you can identify the tree. This is useful when trees are leafless!

Beech

Oak

Lime

Pine

Silver bark of beech, and sallow
Bark of yellow birch and yellow
Twig of willow. Edna St Vincent Millay

The bark of the pine tree and the plane tree comes off in flakes, leaving paler bark underneath.

The birch has silvery bark which peels off like paper. It is used for tanning leather.

All its life the beech has thin, smooth bark which gives the tree little protection. In summer this is provided by a dense covering of leaves that not only protect the tree from the weather but create so much shade that very little undergrowth is found beneath beech trees.

Elms are proud
and cedars dark,
poplars have silver
leaf-shadowed
bark,
aspens whisper,
willows weep,
and all the tree toads
have gone to sleep.
Elizabeth
Coatsworth

Cherry

Maple

Birch

Plane

Seedtime

Seeds are carried by wind, water, birds, animals, even by people, unaware that they have seeds stuck to their shoes or clinging to their clothes.

Ripe autumn fruits drop to the ground. If they are left to rot, the seeds inside them will sink into the earth. In time some of them may germinate and grow. But many seeds travel great distances before this happens.

The more widely seeds are spread, the more likely it is that some of them will reach a place where they can grow. Seeds usually need to get away from the parent plant. In the shadow of an oak an acorn will not get enough sun. But if a squirrel carries it off, buries and then forgets it, in spring the acorn may germinate... and one day grow into a new oak tree.

A dormouse

Big seeds *(acorn, hazelnut)* may be carried away by a squirrel or a field-mouse.

Acorn

Winged seeds *(maple, lime, ash)* spin round in the wind that blows them a short distance.

Lime

Plumed seeds *(dandelion)* can travel for miles on the wind, each seed hanging from its parachute.

Dandelion

Projectile seeds *(broom, honesty)* are thrown out of their pod which bursts open when it is ripe.

Honesty

Hooked seeds *(burdock)* cling to the fur of animals.

Hazelnut

Ash

Maple

Dandelion

Broom

Burdock

Now mushrooms with the morning light
Above the wet grass glisten white.
John Clare

A mushroom does not have leaves, or branches and flowers, but it is still a plant.

The part of the mushroom we see above the ground is the fruit. Underneath there is a network of fine threads called *hyphae*, from which the fruit grows.

The hyphae break down decaying leaves and wood to make food. Another name for plants like mushrooms and toadstools is fungi. Fungi do a good job clearing the ground of dead plants.

Some fungi feed on living wood. One of these is the Dutch Elm disease fungus, which has killed so many elms.

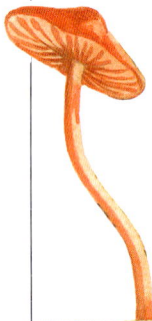

Overnight, very
Whitely, discreetly,
Very quietly
Our toes, our noses
Take hold on the loam.

Sylvia Plath

Mushrooms and toadstools

Mushrooms like to grow where it is warm and moist and the soil is soft, so conditions are best for them in late summer or autumn, after rain.

A new mushroom's cap is tightly buttoned, and so is called a button mushroom. Then the cap opens out to show the *gills* on its underside. The gills are fine ribs, running outwards like the spokes of an umbrella. They give out *spores*: the 'seeds' of the plant. In the space of an hour, one mushroom can give out over 40 million spores. They are invisible and so light that the slightest breeze carries them away.

The air is full of spores of all kinds of fungi which can travel huge distances. The mould that appears on old bread is a kind of fungus.

1 Cap
2 Skin
3 Flesh
4 Gills
5 Ring
6 Stalk

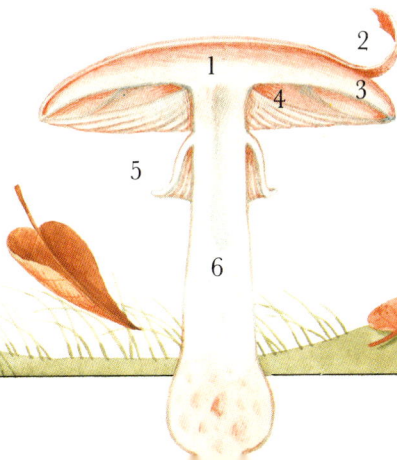

Edible mushrooms

The fungi on these two pages are edible, and some are considered delicacies, but you should never eat any fungus unless you are with an expert who is absolutely certain it is safe.

This is because, for almost every mushroom that is safe to eat, there is a fungus that looks very like it but is dangerous. People die of fungus-poisoning every year.

Fairy ring (1)
Grows in rings in fields. Each year the ring moves outwards by 15 to 30 cm. (6 to 12 in.). Some rings are hundreds of years old.

Cep or 'Penny bun' boletus (2)
Grows in woods and fields. Ceps are often dried then used in small quantities to add a rich flavour to sauces.

Chanterelle (3)
Grows in woods, in moss under dead leaves and pine needles.

Horn of plenty (4)

Grows in woods where the soil is muddy, among dead leaves and wood. Has a lovely smell when fresh.

4

Cultivated mushroom (5)

This is the button mushroom commonly sold in shops. It is usually grown in caves or cellars in specially prepared beds of fine soil and manure.

5

Boletus (6)

There are many kinds of boletus, some of which are not safe to eat. This one, *boletus erythropus*, can be eaten cooked but is poisonous when raw. It grows in woods.

6

Field mushroom (7)

Grows in fields and meadows. It is related to the cultivated mushroom.

7

Fir-cone hydnum (8)

This little fungus grows in woods, under pine needles and sometimes on pine-cones. It can be eaten, but needs to be cooked for a long time.

8

Parasol mushroom (9)

Grows in grassy places, usually near trees. It is delicious to eat, though the stalk may be tough.

9

Poisonous fungi

BEWARE!

There are many kinds of poisonous fungi to be found in woods and fields. These pages show a few of them. Some can kill. Others make people very ill. Be careful: *never touch them*.

1 Volva
2 Ring
3 Gills

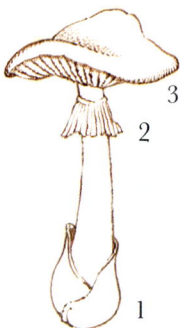

These are some points to look out for:
1. A volva, which is a pocket of skin surrounding the base of the stalk.
2. A ring of pale skin around the stalk.
3. White gills under the cap.

Verdigris toadstool (1)
Found in grassy woods. Its bright blue-green cap fades as it grows older.

The Sickener (2)
It has a bright scarlet cap, and grows in woods, in damp and mossy places.

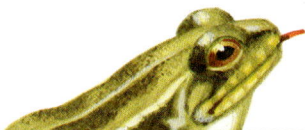

Fairy cake hebeloma (3)
Grows in woods. Its cap is often sticky.

Fly agaric (4)
Grows in woods, especially under birch trees. This is the red and white spotted toadstool often pictured in fairy stories.

The Panther (5)
Similar to the Fly Agaric, only smaller and with a brown or greenish cap.

The Death Cap (6)
The most poisonous known mushroom. Learn to recognise it. Grows in woods, especially in the South and West of England. When mature it has a yellowish-green or light brown cap, but when young it can quite easily be mistaken for a field mushroom. But it has white gills, a white ring attached to the upper half of the stalk, and a loose white volva round its base. **Never touch it.**

The toadstool wood is dark and
mouldy,
And has a ferny smell.
About the trees hangs something
quiet
And queer – like a spell. . .
James Reeves

The autumn morning, waked by many a gun,
Throws o'er the fields her many-coloured light.

John Clare

The sun eases away the last drops of dew,
cows move with their shadows
out of steaming milking sheds,
a flock of gulls dips in from the sea,
settle as one bird along stubbled lines,
a tractor puffs away the morning,
crisp barley gathered in;
a man strides with dog and gun
across the slopes.

Leonard Clark

Shooting season

A long time ago men lived by hunting. With spears or bows and arrows they chased deer and other wild animals. They also dug traps. Later, men became farmers. They grew crops and reared animals where they lived so they no longer had to hunt for meat. Hunting wild animals became a sport, as fishing and shooting have remained today.

Autumn is the shooting season for most game birds: partridge, pheasant, duck and geese, for example. It is against the law to shoot them out of season, when they are breeding.

Rabbits and wood pigeons which are considered pests by the farmer, can be shot at any time of the year.

Run, rabbit run!
Run to your
*   warren!*
The harvest is
*   done,*
The meadow is
*   barren.*
The corn was your
*   shelter*
From stone, stick
*   and gun,*
Heltery, skeltery,
Run, rabbit, run!
    Eleanor Farjeon

Animal camouflage

As winter draws near, the bright coat of the red squirrel darkens to grey on its flanks and legs. The roe deer, normally a reddish brown, turns grey too, from November to March. Both animals are then less noticeable in the grey and leafless woods. They are using camouflage to make it harder for their enemies to see them.

Spotted and mottled coats also help animals to stay hidden against the light and dark patterns of the woods and fields. Most deer have spots when they are young. Fallow deer never lose them.

The hen pheasant has dark markings on her dull brown feathers, so she blends in with the dead leaves on the forest floor as she hunts for seeds and insects. This may save her from the eyes of a hungry fox or stoat.

In a field, the ringed plover would stand out: it has a black collar, black and white markings on its head, a white breast and a sand-coloured body. But the plover lives on the shore, where it blends in with the sand and different-coloured pebbles.

*Under the pines
and hemlocks
So thick
the needles lie
You scarcely hear
The shy, dun deer
With its young
go softly by*
Mary Austin

When autumn's fruit is packed and stored,
And barns are full of corn and grain;
When leaves come tumbling down to earth,
Shot down by wind or drops of rain:
Then up the road we'll whistling go,
And, with a heart that's merry,
We'll rob the squirrel of a nut,
Or chaffinch of a berry.

W.H. Davies

Observing wild life

To observe wild animals, use camouflage as they do: you will be less noticeable if you wear dark clothes and a hat.

Move without a sound. And, when you see something, hide at least 10 metres away, behind a tree trunk or rock. If you are in a field with no cover, lie face down. Keep absolutely still.

Position yourself against the wind: it should blow from the animals towards you. Otherwise they may catch your scent and be scared away.

Evening and early morning are the best times to observe animals. They go out to feed then and are less wary.

In the daytime you can look out for signs of animal life: tracks in the mud or sand; fresh droppings; nests and entrances to underground homes; disturbed or flattened grass, where perhaps an animal lay down. Nibbled branches and stripped bark are signs of deer. But others eat bark too: voles, rabbits, squirrels, sheep . . . each feeding at a different level on the tree.

When you watch
for
Feather or fur
Feather or fur
Do not stir
Do not stir
John Becker

As I went home on the old wood road,
with my basket and lesson book,

A deer came out of the tall trees
And down to drink at the brook.

Twilight was all about us,
Twilight and tree on tree;
I looked straight into its great,
strange eyes,
And the deer looked back at me.

Beautiful, brown, and unafraid,
Those eyes returned my stare;
And something with neither sound
nor name
Passed between us there.

Something I shall not forget –
Something still, and shy, and wise –
In the dimness of the woods
From a pair of gold-flecked
eyes.

Rachel Field

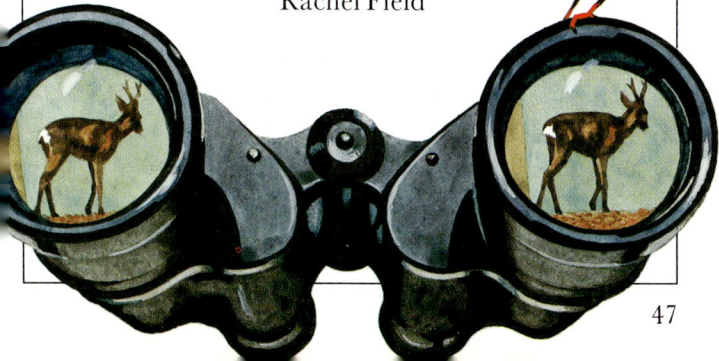

Marsh and woodland

Teal

Snipe

Mallard

The teal is the smallest European duck. From July to October the brightly coloured male is a dull-brown, like the female. This protects him during his annual moult: like many ducks, while he is growing new feathers he cannot fly.

The snipe flies in zig-zags. Some snipe spend all year in Britain. In autumn many more arrive from further north for the winter.

The mallard chooses its mate in the autumn. You may see several drakes chasing one female in the air. Mallard couples spend the winter together and in the new year the female builds a nest for her eggs.

The pheasant lives in woods and fields. It spends the day in the undergrowth and the night perched in a tree. In spring it eats young shoots and grasses; in summer grain, seeds and insects; then, in the autumn, it moves on to a diet of berries, acorns and beech mast.

Pheasant

The woodcock lives in the woods where it is well hidden among dead leaves, thanks to its brown markings. With its long beak it probes for worms and insects in the earth. It can see danger from behind while feeding: eyes set high on its head give it all-round vision.

*The pheasant glows
and gleams
In his finest
autumn plumes.
He is a moving
feast of flame.*
Geoffrey
Summerfield

Woodcock

Field and farmland

Partridge

Quail

The partridge likes to live on farmland, especially where there are hedgerows for cover. It feeds on low plants, grain, seeds and insects. Partridges live in family groups called *coveys*. They roost together, facing outwards to watch for danger.

The quail comes to Britain for the summer and flies to Africa in October. It is a very shy bird and is becoming rare. You are unlikely to see one fly unless a dog has scared it.

Rabbit

The rabbit lives in a network of underground burrows known as a *warren*. It comes out at dusk to feed on grass and other plants, often doing much damage to crops.

The hare, which is a bigger and heavier relation of the rabbit, likes to keep to the open fields where no enemy can approach unseen. It has no burrow to run to, but relies on speed to escape its predators.

Hare

The hare, the hare-kin,
The scutter, the fellow in the dew,
And also the hedge-frisker,
The stag of the stubble, long-eared,
The animal of the stubble, the springer,
The wild animal, the jumper,
The dew-beater, the dew-hopper,
The sitter on its form, the hopper in the grass,
The fidgety-footed one, the sitter on the
ground,
The light-foot, the sitter in the bracken,
The small-tailed one, the one who turns to the
hills,
The white-bellied one.

Old English Poem

Partridge

51

Deer

2 years

3 years

4 years

5 years

From the age of two, male **red deer** grow *antlers*, which are a pair of bony structures that emerge from their foreheads.

Every spring the deer's antlers break off and he grows a new pair during the summer.

The first antlers are like a pair of straight horns. Year by year they grow in size and add more branches until, by the age of five, a deer may have 10 *points*, or *tines*, to each antler.

The growing antlers are covered by a skin known as the *velvet*. It carries the blood the antlers need to grow.

Once the antlers are fully grown, the velvet withers and dies. Deer then rub their antlers against trees to clean off the velvet.

A male red deer is called a *stag*.

Autumn is the deer's mating season, called the *rut*. Each male tries to gather a group of females round him and is ready to fight his rivals with antlers and hooves.

Stags behave strangely at mating time. They sometimes wallow in mud, as a pig might do, and they can be heard roaring out challenges to each other.

*The deer
    which lives
On the evergreen
    mountain
Where there are
    no autumn
leaves
Can know the
    coming
    of autumn
Only by its own
cry.*

Onakatomi
Yoshinobu

Birds of prey

Golden Eagle

Griffon vulture

Kite

Goshawk

Kestrel

Sparrow-hawk

He hangs between his wings outspread
Level and still
And bends a narrow golden head,
Scanning the ground to kill.

Andrew Young

Birds of prey have long, powerful talons, for seizing hold of their prey, and strong, hooked beaks, for tearing at its flesh. They eat small mammals, insects and occasionally other small birds.

Birds of prey use their sharp eyesight to spot their victims. They are strong fliers and some, such as the goshawk and sparrow-hawk, can seize their prey on the wing. The kestrel, on the other hand, hovers over fields while searching the ground below . . . then suddenly pounces on a mouse or rabbit.

Buzzards, less agile than other birds of prey, may sit on a post on the lookout for hours before gliding down on an unwary victim.

Buzzard

Wild berries

During autumn the hedgerows gleam with berries, the fruits of plants, bushes and trees. Some, such as raspberries, blackberries, bilberries and wild strawberries, are delicious eaten as soon as they have been picked. Other edible berries are good to eat only after they have been made into jams, jellies, or liqueurs.

Raspberry

Blackberry

Bilberry

Red Bilberry

Sloe

Wild Strawberry

Rose hip

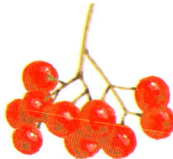

Rowan berries

Juniper berries

In autumn and winter birds will gorge themselves
on berries. They like blackberries, but they can also
eat other berries like rowan, holly or ivy, which would
give people a nasty stomach-ache.

Deadly nightshade

Honeysuckle

Privet

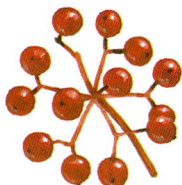

Viburnum

Arum

Black nightshade

Ivy

Virginia creeper

Dogwood

Spindle tree

Holly

Solomon's seal

On the riverbank

Water voles are active in the daytime. Look out for signs of their presence: plants that have been nibbled or bitten off; holes in the bank; the 'plop' of the vole diving into the water when alarmed.

In a hole in the bank of a pond or river the **water vole** rests during spells of cold weather. The entrance to its burrow is often under water, with a shaft leading up through the river bank for air. Sometimes it stores food such as acorns, hazel and beech nuts, there.

The water vole is an excellent swimmer. It usually swims under the water and will even go under the ice. Its fur is waterproof and special valves close its ears to keep out the water.

The water vole, often mistakenly called a water rat, is the largest vole in Europe apart from the *musk rat*: really another vole, which was brought over from North America to be farmed for its fur.

A musk rat swimming

I heard the grey leaves weep
And whisper round my bed,
The river singing, singing,
Singing through my head.

James Reeves

Some musk rats escaped into the wild and the species has spread over much of the Continent. But it is not now found in England.

The musk rat can be twice as large as the water vole and tends to swim on the surface of the water. Both these animals feed on reeds, rushes and other water plants and sometimes on insects and shellfish. They build platforms out of twigs and like to sit on them to feed or groom their fur.

Water vole

The kingfisher

F was once a little
* fish,*
Fishy
Wishy
Squishy
Fishy
In a Dishy
          Edward Lear

The brilliantly coloured kingfisher lives by lakes and streams. It perches nearby, motionless, looking for fish; then suddenly dives, spears one with its sharp, dagger-like bill and surges out of the water again bearing its catch.

Back on its perch, the kingfisher beats the fish against a branch then swallows it head first. If swallowed tail first, the fish's scales and fins would open outwards, choking the bird.

Sometimes the kingfisher misses the fish and has to try again. It needs to eat about six fish a day.

When the water freezes, kingfishers have a hard time. Their prey is under the ice. Some birds go to the coast to look for food, or move towards the south. Many of them die.

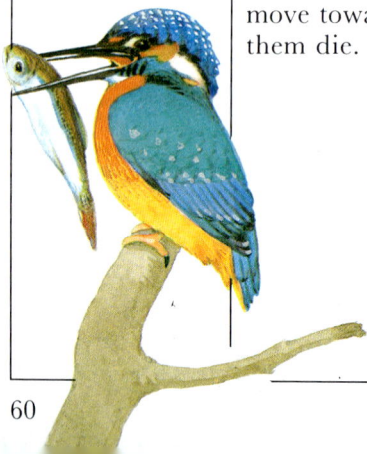

I know a deep and lonely pool
  – that's where
The great Kingfisher
  makes his sudden splash:
He has so many jewels
  in his plumes
That all we see is
  one blue lightning flash.

W.H. Davies

The eel's extraordinary journey

The development of an eel larva

Towards the end of October, eels set out on a long journey. They leave the streams and rivers of Britain and head out across the Atlantic Ocean towards the Sargasso Sea, just this side of the West Indies.

Those eels that manage to reach the Sargasso lay their eggs there and die. They will never return to fresh water.

Tiny larvae hatch from the eggs and start to swim back towards the rivers from which their parents came. This journey takes them three years.

Sargasso Sea

By the time they arrive, they have grown into *elvers:* transparent little eels, about 7 cm long.

Elvers reach the British coast in large numbers in the spring. They swim up rivers, streams, ditches, canals, and arrive at muddy ponds. There they feed on little fishes, seeds and insects and grow into adults.

When the eels are 10 to 15 years old they leave fresh water and set out one autumn day, as their parents did, towards the Sargasso Sea.

Elver

I don't mind eels
Except at meals.
And the way they
feels.

Ogden Nash

Huge numbers of birds migrate in late summer and autumn, often travelling thousands of kilometres to spend the winter in warmer lands.

Well before the cold weather arrives, these birds know that winter lies ahead and they get ready to leave. They build up stores of fat in preparation for their journey. Some birds double their weight before they migrate.

Swallows, swifts, house martins, cuckoos and turtle-doves are just a few of the birds that leave Britain to escape the winter. They head mostly for Africa. Many die on the way. But those that arrive will be sure of a plentiful food supply: it will be spring in Africa, with insects multiplying and plants growing.

When spring comes to Britain again, the birds will return.

Swallow

Migrating birds

As some birds leave Britain to go further south, others arrive from the north to spend the winter.

Wild geese and ducks, gulls, finches, starlings, kestrels, snipe and blackbirds are among these winter visitors. They join other birds of their own species who live in Britain all year round. As soon as spring comes, they will return to the north to breed. The snows will have melted and there will be food again in plenty.

Sometimes a rare visitor will appear in the autumn, such as a stork straying on its journey from Continental Europe to Africa.

Black-headed gull

Stork

Wild goose

Wild geese,
wild geese,
ganging to the sea,
Good weather
it will be;

Wild geese,
wild geese,
ganging to the hill,
The weather
it will spill.

                    Anon.

Birds travel to the same place every year. They are born with the instinct to migrate there. Young cuckoos migrate on their own, some weeks after the adults. They fly instinctively to Africa, where they have never been before!

Mallard
(wild duck)

Migrating birds may use the sun and stars to guide them or, it has been suggested, have their own kind of radar. Swifts and swallows travel by day. They feed as they fly, catching insects in the air.

Many birds travel at night, invisible to us. Sometimes on a starry autumn night you can hear the cry of geese overhead. In some way not yet quite understood birds can navigate by starlight and moonlight with amazing skill.

Swift

Blue tits and wood pigeons are here all year. Sometimes tits from the continent visit southern England. And pigeons from Scandinavia move south in winter.

How fast do they fly?
A swift can fly at 100 km/h.
A duck between 80 and 90 km/h.
A goose at 60 km/h.
Tits and sparrows fly at 30 km/h.

How high do they fly?
Finches fly at 200m.
Wood pigeons between 800 and 2400m.
Sparrows over 1500m.
Swifts can fly so high we cannot see them, while teal and geese can fly over high mountains. (In comparison, Ben Nevis is just over 1200m.)

How far can they fly?
Some birds can fly 200 to 600 km in a day; others only go 100 km in a fortnight. The American Golden Plover can fly over 300km non-stop across the Atlantic from the Arctic to South America.

Something told the wild geese
It was time to go.
Though the field lay golden
Something whispered, 'Snow.'
                              Rachel Field

Blue tits

Wood pigeons

Autumn flowers

Aster

The last flowers of the year bloom in autumn gardens, before they can be nipped by the frost. They attract late butterflies as well as bees that will soon be feeding on the honey they have stored.

Dahlia

Sneezeweed

Fuschia

Hibiscus

Cyclamen

Pampas grass

The gentian's bluest fringes
Are curling in the sun;
In dusty pods the milkweed
Its hidden silk has spun.

The sedges flaunt their harvest,
In every meadow-nook;
And asters by the brookside
Make asters in the brook.

By all these lovely tokens
September days are here,
With summer's best of wealth
And autumn's best of cheer.

Helen Hunt Jackson

Chrysanthemum

Cinquefoil   Marigold   Foxglove

Life at a snail's pace

Snails love drizzle. They come out of their shells only when there is plenty of moisture around, especially at night.

Snails hide from the sun to protect their skin, which dries out very easily. In dry weather snails can seal themselves into their shells, or attach themselves to plants and wait for rain.

At the first signs of cold weather, in September or October, the snail digs a burrow in the earth, seals itself into its shell and goes to sleep until the spring.

Snails are a favourite food of the thrush, which holds the snail's shell in its beak and cracks it open against a stone.

You never heard a snail in song? Wait till the first thrush comes along.

Ralph Hodgson

Little snail,
Dreaming you go.
Weather and rose
Is all you know.

Weather and rose
Is all you see,
Drinking
The dewdrop's
Mystery.

Langston Hughes

A calendar of vegetables

Celery, raw,
Develops the jaw,
But celery stewed,
Is more quietly
chewed.
Ogden Nash

There is still plenty to be picked in the September vegetable garden. There are potatoes to be dug up and put into bags, and onions to be tied in bundles. They will both keep into the winter.

	September	October	November
 Artichokes			
 Celery			
 Cucumber			
 Leeks			
 Beetroot			
 Onions			
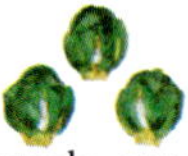 Brussels sprouts			

	to be picked		to be sown
 to be picked		 to be sown	

When November comes, it is time to dig the garden over and burn dead leaves and garden rubbish. Gardeners prepare seedbeds under glass frames for the lettuces that will grow in the spring.

Eat some spinach and you'll turn green (I'm not saying that it's true But that's what I heard, and so I thought I'd pass it on to you.)
Shel Silverstein

September	October	November	
			 Peas
			 Potatoes
			 Cabbage
Can be sown and picked all year			 Spinach
			 Carrots
			 Cauliflowers
			Turnips

Autumn fruit

Plums

Golden plum

Greengage

Damson

Yellow gage

Birds and insects are often the first to taste the ripening autumn fruit. Wasps are particularly hungry for sweet foods: the wasp grubs that produced a sweet liquid for them in the summer have grown into wasps themselves.

Pears

Comice

Conference

Figs

The gold scales of heaven
See how they swing
With fruits of the fall
That were flowers in the spring.
                    Eleanor Farjeon

Pears

Louise Bonne

William's

Beurré Hardy

Nuts

Walnut

Almond

Hazelnut

Chestnut

75

Apples

*Rosy the blossom
that breaks in May;
Autumn brings
the apple.*
Walter de La Mare

Crab apple

There are many more kinds of apple than we ever see in the shops. Apple-growers choose those that best resist disease and insects and that keep and travel well after picking.

Apples will keep through the winter if they are properly stored: on racks, not touching each other, in a cool, dark, dry place.

Apples left on the ground provide a feast for the insect world. Woodlice will eat away until nothing remains but the apple skin.

Worcester

Russet

Golden Delicious

Starking

Boskop

Granny Smith

Cider

Until this century nearly all cider was made on the farm. Cider mills worked by a horse or ox pulling a stone wheel which turned in a stone tub, crushing the apples. The apple pulp was pressed to extract all the juice, which was then poured into barrels to ferment.

Nowadays most cider is made by machines and sold in shops. But there are still people who make their own, in parts of Devon for example.

What is fermentation?

Fermentation is a process that turns apple juice into cider and grape juice into wine. It is caused by yeast, a fungus found on the skin of fruit. Yeast turns the sugar in fruit into alcohol and carbon dioxide.

For sweet wines and ciders, fermentation is interrupted and extra sugar may be added.

When the fruit juice is left to ferment completely, all the sugar turns into alcohol and carbon dioxide: the wine or cider is then 'dry', meaning not sweet.

Amy Elizabeth Ermyntrude Annie
Went to the country to visit her Grannie,

Learnt to churn butter and learnt to make cheese,
Learnt to milk cows and take honey from bees,

Learnt to spice rose-leaves and learnt to cure ham,
Learnt to make cider and blackcurrant jam.

Queenie Scott Hopper

Grapes to eat and drink

Grapes can be eaten fresh or dried to make raisins. Oil is made out of grape seeds. And dye is extracted from grape skins: this is the purple dye often used to stamp meat. But many varieties are grown especially for wine-making.

Wine grapes

Cabernet franc

Cabernet sauvignon

Gamay

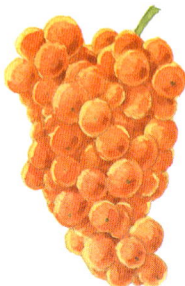

Chardonnay

Roussanne

Sauvignon

Grapes grow best in warm, sunny climates, and fermentation will not work properly if there has been much rain shortly before the harvest, as much of the yeast will have been washed off the grape skins. For this reason, Mediterranean countries have been much more successful than countries with colder climates, such as Britain, at producing wine.

Grapes for eating

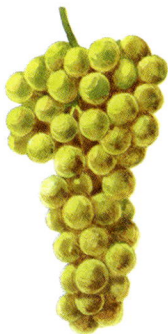

Chasselas   White muscat   Gros-vert

Alphonse-Lavalée   Black muscat   Frankhental

Grape growing

Grapes grow on vines, which are climbing plants like ivy, and need support. They are generally planted in rows secured to a line of stakes linked by wires, or they grow up trellises.

Vineyards need attention all year round. In winter the soil is ploughed and fertilised. Before the sap rises in spring each vine is pruned: weaker shoots are cut back so that the sap will feed the stronger shoots, which will produce more grapes. In late spring clusters of small greenish flowers open on the vine. When their petals fall, they start to develop into the grapes which will be harvested in autumn.

In the months between the earth must be weeded; and the growing fruit sprayed with special products to protect it from diseases. Grapes are generally left on the vine until October. They need plenty of sun to ripen, especially in the weeks before they are picked. The fruit is cut in bunches with special knives. It must be handled with great care.

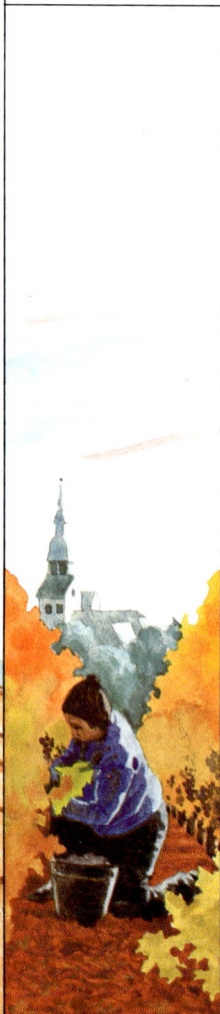

Man has been growing grapes for wine for at least 6000 years and probably longer. The cultivation of the grape spread to Western Europe from the Middle or Near East. It was brought to France and Britain by the Romans: their soldiers liked to drink wine and planted vineyards in the countries they occupied. Most of the vineyards in Europe today were there in Roman times.

From Europe explorers and missionaries took the grape to other continents. It now grows in places as far apart as Australia, California, South Africa, Chile and Argentina, the USSR and China as well as the countries surrounding the Mediterranean.

Wine

After harvest grapes are taken straight to pressing houses.

After pressing, the grape juice, known as *must*, is left in vats or casks to ferment.

Red wine is made out of black grapes. The skins are left in the must during fermentation. This gives the wine its colour.

White wine can be made from either black or white grapes. It is pressed and fermented in the same way as for red wine, but then the skins are taken out and the must keeps a light colour.

To make rosé wine, the skins are left in the juice just long enough to colour it slightly.

The fermented juice, now wine, is left to mature in barrels in cellars. It forms deposits which need to be removed. The wine is filtered as well to make it clear. Finally it is put in bottles and is ready for the shops.

Grapes used to be pressed by people treading on them in bare feet.

84

France grows more grapes and produces more wine than any other country. The English climate is not so well suited to the grape. But vineyards were successfully cultivated in Roman times and through the middle ages. There was even a vineyard at Westminster in London. And in the last thirty years people have returned to growing grapes in England and making English wine.

Oh, some are fond
of red wine,
and some are fond
of white,
And some
are all for dancing
by the pale moonlight.

John Masefield

A Vagabond Song

There is something in the autumn that is native
to my blood –
Touch of manner, hint of mood;
And my heart is like a rhyme,
With the yellow and the purple and the crimson
keeping time.

The scarlet of the maples can shake me like a cry
Of bugles going by.
And my lonely spirit thrills
To see the frosty asters like a smoke upon the
hills.

There is something in October sets the gypsy
blood astir;
We must rise and follow her,
When from every hill of flame
She calls and calls each vagabond by name.

Bliss Carman

Autumn alphabet

Advent
The four weeks leading up to Christmas are known as Advent, which means 'coming'.

Bats
Bats are the only mammals that fly. In cold weather they hibernate, hanging upside down in a barn or hollow tree, their wings folded round them.

Bees
In autumn the male bees, called drones, are driven from the hive by the female workers. The drones, who did no work in the summer, die in the cold. The queen and workers spend the winter in the hive feeding on honey.

First I am frosted
Second I am beaten
Third I am roasted
Fourth I am eaten.

Chestnut

Conkers
Hobbley, hobbley
*   onker,*
My first conker,
Hobbley hobbley
*   ho,*
My first go.
                    Anon.

Conkers is an old game played with chestnuts on strings: each player tries to crack the other's nut. The word 'conker' comes from 'conquer'. The game was originally played with snail shells.

Deadly Nightshade
The black berries of this plant are poisonous enough to kill anyone who eats them.

Eider
Eider ducks live on the north coast of Britain. But ice may drive them south. The female lines her nest with

87

down from her breast. In some countries people use this down as filling for quilts or 'eider-downs'.

Fire
When we light fires and lanterns at Hallowe'en and Guy Fawkes Night, we are continuing a custom that is older than Christianity.

Grey seal
Grey seals found along the west coast of Britain, have their pups in autumn. The young feed for a few weeks on their mother's milk then learn to fish and fend for themselves.

Hallowe'en
Once people believed that the dead came back to visit their families at Hallowe'en, so food was put on the table for them.

Indian summer
A short spell of hot weather which occurs in late autumn.

Jack O' Lantern
A mysterious light which flickers in marshy places on warm summer or autumn evenings.

Keys
The fruits of the ash tree are known as keys.

Ashtree, ashtree, throw me if you please,
Throw me down a slender bunch of russet-gold keys.
Rose Fyleman

Leaves
Before leaves die, they make sugar for the tree to feed on in winter. But on very cold nights they cannot pass the sugar to the tree. It collects in the dying leaves, giving them their brilliant red and gold colours.

Mischief night

An old name for Hallowe'en.

Northern lights

The spring and autumn equinoxes are good times to see the northern lights or Aurora Borealis. They are streams of light which appear in the night sky, sometimes in brilliant colours but more often whitish.

Otter

The shy and now rare otter may breed at this time of year. Its nest is a hole in the riverbank or under the roots of a tree. Otters are good swimmers and can close their ears and nostrils under water, where they catch fish and frogs.

Poison pie

This poisonous mushroom is also known as fairy cake. It has a brownish cap on a whitish stem and grows in wooded places.

Poppy

The seed pod of the poppy is like a little jar with holes at the top. When the pod moves in the wind, the seeds are thrown out.

Queen wasp

The queen is the only wasp to survive the winter. The others all die when cold weather comes.

Remembrance Sunday

The Sunday nearest to 11 November is set aside in memory of all who died in the two World Wars.

Sedge warbler

This little brown bird goes to Africa in September, flying for four days and nights without stopping.

Thanksgiving

Thanksgiving, a national holiday in the USA. The first Thanksgiving after harvest was celebrated in 1621 by the Pilgrim Fathers, who had come from England to settle in America.

Ursa Major and Ursa Minor

These constellations, also known as the Great and Little Bear, can be seen clearly in the autumn sky and are known as circumpolar stars.

Vegetable beefsteak

This edible mushroom grows on living trees, especially oaks, often high up out of reach.

As soft as silk,
As white as milk,
As bitter as gall.
A thick wall
And a green coat
covers me all.
Walnut

X

X is the Roman number ten. October is the tenth month of our year. But it gets its name from 'octo', the Latin word for eight, because it was the eighth month in the Roman calendar.

Yellowhammer

Yellowhammers migrate to Britain from the Continent in autumn.

Zelkova

This is an unusual tree, related to the elm. It bears small nuts in the autumn.

Biographies

Laurence Ottenheimer taught history and geography for a few years before working in publishing, where she specialises in activity and information books for young children. She loves the natural world and the outdoor life and has just completed a book about mountains.

Henri Galeron, the illustrator of *Autumn,* was born in 1939 in a village in Provence in the sunny South of France. He studied art in Marseilles and had his first book published in 1973. Since then he has never stopped working, illustrating innumerable children's books, book covers, record sleeves, and posters. An extremely well-known and highly-regarded illustrator in France, he now lives near Paris with his wife and young children.

Alex Campbell studied English Literature at Oxford. Now the mother of two young children, she enjoys working on children's books while they are at school. In her work on the four *Discoverers* Season books she has taken particular pleasure in the choosing of the poems.

Acknowledgements

The editor and publisher wish to thank the following for permission to use copyright material:

Alfred A. Knopf Inc. for *Snail* by Langston Hughes from Fields of Wonder; George Allen and Unwin Ltd. and Arthur Waley for *Autumn wind rises . . .* by Emperor Wu-Ti, trans. Arthur Waley; Jonathan Cape Ltd. for *The Fog, The One Singer, P is for Pool, Plants and Men, When Autumn's Fruit* by W.H. Davies from Complete Poems; the Author for *Song* by Elizabeth Coatsworth; William Collins Sons & Co. Ltd. for *Remembrance* by Eleanor Farjeon from All the Year Round; the Author for *November Night* by Adelaide Crapsey; Faber and Faber Ltd. for *I never see the stars at night* by George Barker from Aylsham Fair and for *Hallowe'en Pumpkin* by Dorothy Aldis from The Book of Nursery Verse; Dennis Dobson Ltd. for *English Country* by Leonard Clark in The Broad Atlantic; André Deutsch Ltd. for *Hot and Cold, Season of Sport* by Geoffrey Summerfield from Welcome and Other Poems; Doubleday Inc. for *The Mist and All* by Dixie Wilson from Favourite Poems Old and New, ed. Helen Ferris; the Author for *October* by Rose Fyleman; Harper and Row Inc. for *Fall Wind* by Aileen Fisher from Out in the Dark and Daylight; William Heinemann Ltd. for *Boating, The Toadstool Wood* by James Reeves; and for *Now it is autumn and the falling fruit . . .* by D.H. Lawrence from Complete Poems; Hodder & Stoughton Ltd. for *Trees* by Leonard Clark from The Singing Time; Houghton Mifflin Co. for *The Deer* by Mary Austin from The Children Sing in the Forest; Olwyn Hughes for *Mushrooms* by Sylvia Plath from The Colossus, published by Faber and Faber, © Ted Hughes 1967; Michael Joseph Ltd. for *This is the week* by Eleanor Farjeon from Silver Sand and Snow; J.B. Lippincott Co. for *Joan's Door* by Eleanor Farjeon; The Literary Trustees of Walter de la Mare for *Apple Fall* by Walter de la Mare from Collected Rhymes and Verses; Little, Brown & Co. for *Celery, I don't mind . . .* by Ogden Nash from Parents Keep Out; Lothrop, Lee & Shepherd Co. for *The geese flying . . .* by Sally Andresen from Reflections on a Gift of Watermelon Pickle and Other Modern Verse (ed. S. Dunning et al.); Macmillan & Co. Ltd. for *The Snail* by Ralph Hodgson from Collected Poems; and for *Day by Day* from This Way Winter by James Stephens; Macmillan Publishing Co. Inc., New York, for *Meeting, Something Told the Wild Geese* by Rachel Field from Poems; Methuen Publishers Ltd. for *Vegetables* by Shel Silverstein from Oh that's ridiculous; Oxford University Press Ltd. for *Heltery Skeltery, Libra* by Eleanor Farjeon from The Children's Bells; Pantheon Books Ltd. for *When you watch . . .* by John Becker from New Feathers for the Old Goose; Secker & Warburg Ltd. and the Author's estate for *Late Autumn* by Andrew Young from Complete Poems; The Society of Authors for *Captain Stratton's Fancy* by John Masefield; Arthur Waley for his translation of *River-fog* by Fukayaba Kiyowara.

Every effort has been made to trace copyright but if any omissions have been made please let us know in order that we may put it right in the next edition.